ABUNDANT TRUTH INTERNATIONAL MINISTRIES

Biblical Studies Series

I Will Open My Mouth in Parables

Examining the Parables of the Hidden Treasure and of the Unmerciful Servant

Roderick Levi Evans

P.O. Box 126, Camden, NC 27921

I Will Open My Mouth In Parables

Examining the Parables of the Hidden Treasure and of the Unmerciful Servant

All Rights Reserved ©2009 by Roderick L. Evans

No part of this book may be reproduced or transmitted in any form or by any means, graphic, electronic, or mechanical, including photocopying, recording, taping, or by any information storage or retrieval system, without the permission in writing from the publisher.

Front & Back Cover Designs by Abundant Truth Publishing
Image by **Alana Jordan** from Pixabay

Abundant Truth Publishing
an imprint of Abundant Truth International Ministries

For information address:
Abundant Truth International
P.O. Box 126
Camden, NC 27921

Unless otherwise indicated, all of the scripture quotations are taken from th*e Authorized King James Version* of the Bible. Scripture quotations marked with NIV are taken from the *New International Version* of the Bible. Scripture quotations marked with NASV are taken from the *New American Standard Version* of the Bible. Scripture quotations marked with Amplified are taken from the *Amplified Bible*.

ISBN 13978-1-60141-504-2
Printed in the United States of America.

Contents

Introduction

Study 1 – The Hidden Treasure and Pearl of Great Price   1

Lesson 1 - What Do You Value?   3
The Value of the Kingdom   5
Jesus' Teaching   7

Lesson 2 - The Value of the Hidden Treasure   13
Kingdom of Heaven   16
Treasure Hid in Field   18
Found & Hideth   23
For Joy Selleth and Buyeth   25

Contents (cont.)

Lesson 3 - The Value of the Pearl of Great Price   31

Kingdom of Heaven   34
Merchant Man Seeking Goodly Pearls 35
Found One Pearl of Great Price   39
Sold All and Bought   41

Lesson 4 - The Value of the Kingdom of God   47

Salvation   49
Eternal Life   51
Freedom from Sin   51
Righteousness   53
Joy   55
Peace   57
Power   58

Contents (cont.)

Study 2 – The Unmerciful Servant   63

Lesson 1 - The Choice   65
The Obvious Choice   67
The Overwhelming Command   71

Lesson 2 - The Characters   79
The King   81
The Servant   83
The Fellowservant   85
The Other Fellowservants   87
The Tormentors   89

Lesson 3 - The Circumstances   95
The Call   97
The Cry   101
The Compassion   103

Contents (cont.)

The Corruption	106
The Capture	112
Lesson 4 - The Conclusion	**119**
God's Standard for Forgiveness	121
Man's Reasons for Unforgiveness	122
Bibliography	**133**

Introduction

Paul instructed Timothy to rightly divide the Word of Truth. In order to do this as believers we should follow this example and become students of the Bible. The Biblical Studies Series was developed to aid believers in the study of the various scriptures and foundational doctrines.

In this publication:

Story telling is an age-old tradition used to teach lessons. Stories are sometimes referred to as myths, fables, riddles, epics, and the like. In both Jewish and Christian tradition, when individuals wanted to **explain a spiritual truth**, they used stories known as **parables**.

During His earthly ministry, Jesus primarily used parables to instruct His listeners. In fulfillment of Old Testament prophecy, He taught the people truths concerning the Kingdom of God.

In this study, we will examine the

three parables of the hidden treasure, the pearl of great price, and the unmerciful servant. The first two parables describe the value of the kingdom of God (Matthew 13:44-46).

When we come to know Christ, nothing in this life compares to Him. Our relationship with Him has to take precedence over everything else. Learn of the worth of salvation and the kingdom of heaven. It is a hidden treasure and pearl of great price.

The third parable describes the parable of the unmerciful servant. This parable expresses the responsibility of the believer to forgive (Matthew 18:21-35). When Peter asked Christ about forgiveness, He responded to him with this parable.

Within this story, we see the unlimited forgiveness of God. In addition, we discover the responsibility of His servants to be like Him. Let us learn to forgive others as God, for Christ's sake, forgave us. As we learn from these parables, we will stay on the path to true discipleship.

I Will Open My Mouth in Parables

-Study 1-
The Hidden Treasure and Pearl of Great Price

(Lessons of the Value of the Kingdom)

I Will Open My Mouth in Parables

I Will Open My Mouth in Parables

-Lesson 1-
What Do You Value?

I Will Open My Mouth in Parables

What do you value most in this life? Is it your family? Your job? Your social status? Your possessions? Your ministry? Whatever is valuable to you, you will protect it and work to keep it.

As Christians, we have to ask ourselves about the value of our relationship with Christ. Do we really value the work of Christ on the cross and our place in His Kingdom?

The Value of the Kingdom

If the kingdom of God is not the most valuable possession in our lives, we will not live as we should as Christians.

For where your treasure is, there will your heart be also. (Matthew 6:21)

If the things of this life are most valuable to us, then our attention will be on earthly things. However, if the kingdom the most valuable possession or treasure we have, our attention will be upon Christ and His kingdom.

Again, what do you value in this life? As Christians, we know what to say. With our mouths we speak of how Christ is the best thing in our lives and that He is our everything.

Yet, daily we pursue earthly materials and pleasures above seeking His face and His will for our lives. Is the kingdom of God through Christ valuable to us? Do we really recognize the worth of the kingdom of God?

Jesus' Teaching

While teaching the multitudes, Jesus used a series of parables in Matthew 13. The parables were designed to bring those who heard them into an understanding of different aspects of the kingdom.

In the middle of His parables, He used two parables to describe the value or worth of the kingdom of God.

> *Again, the kingdom of heaven is like unto treasure hid in a field; the which when a man hath found, he hideth, and for joy thereof goeth and selleth all that he hath, and buyeth that field. (Matthew 13:44)*
>
> *Again, the kingdom of heaven is like unto a merchant man, seeking goodly pearls: Who, when he had found one pearl of great price, went and sold all that he had, and bought it. (Matthew 13:45-46)*

These two parables taught the intrinsic value of the kingdom of God. As they are examined, we pray the believer's appreciation of the kingdom grows.

I Will Open My Mouth in Parables

Notes:

I Will Open My Mouth in Parables

-Lesson 2-
The Value of the Hidden Treasure

I Will Open My Mouth in Parables

After speaking of the coming of the Son of man and the judgment of the kingdom of God, Jesus begins to teach on the value of the kingdom.

> *Again, the kingdom of heaven is like unto treasure hid in a field; the which when a man hath found, he hideth, and for joy thereof goeth and selleth all that he hath, and buyeth that field. (Matthew 13:44)*

He likens the kingdom of heaven unto a hidden treasure in a field. A man finds it, hides it, sells all, and buys the field. Though the parable is only one verse, it contains many elements that teach us about the worth of the kingdom.

The key elements (or words) in this parable are *kingdom of heaven*, *treasure*, *hid*, *field*, *found*, *hideth*, *joy*, *selleth*, and *buyeth*. As we examine each element, the worth of the kingdom and our response as partakers of it will be established.

Kingdom of Heaven

To begin most of His parables, Jesus used the phrases 'kingdom of heaven' or 'kingdom of God' to introduce the subject of the parable. His use of this is not coincidental. It is deliberate. Without question, He is establishing how the kingdom of God operates. He wants the listeners to understand that He is not speaking of earthly things, but of spiritual things.

The parable begins with Jesus comparing the kingdom of heaven to a hidden treasure.

Again, the kingdom of heaven is like unto treasure... (Matthew 13:44a)

Therefore, every reference in the parable to the treasure should be noted as a representation of the kingdom of heaven.

Treasure Hid in Field

Having established that the kingdom of heaven is like a hidden treasure, Jesus continues to describe the location of this treasure. He places this treasure as hidden in the field as opposed to any other physical location.

From this, we discover some biblical truths concerning the kingdom of heaven.

Field – The use of field is not a coincidence. The field represents the earth and things of the earth. When God wanted to bring men into the kingdom, He sent Christ in the flesh, which is made up of earth.

Though Christ was visible to all, everyone did not perceive the treasure that was within him. The gift of God (treasure) within Him was in fact hidden.

He was in the world, and the world was made by him, and the world knew him not. He came unto his own, and his own received him not. (John 1:10-11)

John states that He was in the world, but the world did not know Him. The Jews expected Him to come in other ways and do certain things, so the treasure of their redemption (the kingdom) was there, but hidden.

But we preach Christ crucified, unto the Jews a stumbling block, and u the Greeks foolishness. (I Corinthians 1:23)

Jesus describes the treasure as hidden in the field. This means that it was not readily seen though it existed. The kingdom of heaven is all around, but many walk over it as they would treasure buried in a field. Jesus was trying to bring the hearers to understand that the kingdom was there, they only had to go beyond what they saw.

The field is a representation of Christ's physical form, but it also describes the heart of man. The scriptures declare that men are without excuse because God hath shown them who He is.

Because that which may be known of God is manifest in them; for God hath shewed it unto them. For the invisible things of himfrom the creation of the world are clearly seen, being understood by the things that are made, even his eternal power and

> *Godhead; so that they are without excuse. (Romans 1:19-20)*

Through creation, the Lord reveals His glory. However, as the treasure is hidden in the field, man hides the knowledge of God through unrighteousness.

> *For the wrath of God is revealed from heaven against all ungodliness and unrighteousness of men, who hold the truth in unrighteousness. (Romans 1:18)*

The above verse states that men hold (which means to suppress) the knowledge of God. Thus, the knowledge of the kingdom is within man's reach, but because of sin and fleshly desires, it becomes a hidden treasure waiting to be discovered.

Found & Hideth

In the parable, after the man found the hidden treasure, he hides it.

...the which when a man hath found, he hideth. (Matthew 13:44b)

This part of the parable introduces us to the response we must have after receiving Christ and His kingdom. The man hid the discovered treasure. David echoes this sentiment in the Psalms,

> *Thy word have I hid in mine heart, that I might not sin against thee. (Psalm 119:11)*

In order to enter into the kingdom, one has to believe on the name of Jesus. Moreover, the scriptures declare that Jesus is the Word.

> *In the beginning was the Word, and the Word was with God, and the Word was God. (John 1:1)*

Thus, as the man hid the treasure, we have to keep Jesus and His commands in our hearts. He and His word have to be hidden in the depths of our being.

When we understand the worth of the kingdom of God, we will not let sin, unrighteousness, and the world steal the seed of the word of God from us, which is Christ.

The man in the parable understood the value of the hidden treasure; the Christian also has to understand the value of the treasure of the kingdom.

For Joy Selleth and Buyeth

The man in the parable not only responded by hiding the treasure, but he was full of gratitude and joy. Because of his joy, he sold all that he had and bought the field which contained the treasure.

...and for joy thereof goeth and selleth all that he hath, and buyeth tha field. (Matthew 13:44c)

As recipients of God's salvation, the Christian should be willing to sell all that he has in order to gain Christ. This demonstrates that he understands the value of the kingdom. The Christian 'sells all' by becoming willing to give anything up in order to serve the Lord. Paul expresses this same sentiment in his letters to the Philippians.

But what things were gain to me, those I counted loss for Christ. Yea doubtless, and I count all things but loss for the excellency of the knowledge of Christ Jesus my Lord: for whom I have suffered the loss of all things, and do count them but dung, that I may win Christ. (Philippians 3:7-8)

Because of the excellency (richness or greatness) of Christ, Paul claims that all else is nothing more than waste.

When we understand the worth of the kingdom, our outlook on what is valuable and important changes. Everything in this life should pale in comparison to Christ and the kingdom of God.

Notes:

I Will Open My Mouth in Parables

-Lesson 3-
The Value of the Pearl of Great Price

I Will Open My Mouth in Parables

After the parable of the hidden treasure, Jesus emphasized its message by telling another parable. Instead of speaking of an unknown treasure, He used a specific item of value. He called it the pearl of great price.

Again, the kingdom of heaven is like unto a merchant man seeking goodly pearls: Who, when he had found one pearl of great price, went and sold all that he had, and bought it. (Matthew 13:45-46)

As with the first parable, there are key terms and elements that have to be explored. In doing so, we can understand Jesus' message.

The key terms are *kingdom of heaven, merchant man seeking goodly pearls, found one pearl of great price, sold all* and *bought*. As we explore each of these, Jesus' message of the worth of the kingdom is clearly seen.

Kingdom of Heaven

As with the first parable, Jesus identifies the kingdom of heaven as the subject of the parable. It is understood that anytime when Jesus spoke of the kingdom of heaven, He spoke of God's rule, reign, and Sovereignty.

It points to His influence and control. The believers allow God's kingdom to be established as they submit to Him. Again, Jesus compares the kingdom to a pearl of great price.

Merchant Man Seeking Goodly Pearls

Jesus said that the kingdom was like a merchant man seeking goodly pearls. This opens up some vital points. Jesus referred to the man as a merchant.

In biblical times, merchants oftentimes functioned more like tradesmen. They would gather items in order to trade or barter for something else.

> *Again, the kingdom of heaven is like unto a merchant man, seeking goodly pearls. (Matthew 13:45)*

This symbolizes man's constant search in this life for fulfillment. Often times, man will trade his dignity and self-respect for brief moments of fulfillment.

However, his search does not end. Sadly, man's quest (at times) for self-fulfillment ends with eternal death.

> *For whosoever will save his life shall lose it: and whosoever will lose his*

life for my sake shall find it. For what is a man profited, if he shall gain the whole world, and lose his own soul? or what shall a man give in exchange for his soul? (Matthew 16:25- 26)

Jesus' key figure was a merchant man with a specific item in mind. He sought after goodly pearls. Again, Jesus' use of the pearl as the object of desire is no coincidence.

From biblical symbolism, it is understood that pearls represent wisdom. When Jesus spoke of the message of the kingdom and spiritual truths, he used pearls to describe it.

> *Give not that which is holy unto the dogs, neither cast ye your pearls before swine, lest they trample them under their feet, and turn again and rend you. (Matthew 7:6)*

This implies that man searches for knowledge; more specifically, the knowledge of God.

The merchant sought goodly pearls. No doubt, this merchant probably had collected some pearls already. Man collects knowledge and wisdom in his life.

It does not compare to the knowledge of the Lord.

> *The fear of the Lord is the beginning of wisdom: and the knowledge of the holy is understanding. (Proverbs 9:10)*
>
> *The fear of the Lord is the beginning of knowledge: but fools despise wisdom and instruction. (Proverbs 1:7)*

The ultimate truth is the knowledge of God. True wisdom begins with the fear of the Lord.

Found One Pearl of Great Price

As Jesus continued the parable, the

merchant man found one pearl of great price. Jesus gives no monetary value to the pearl or to the amount that the man paid for it. It is because no price can be placed upon the kingdom of heaven.

Who, when he had found one pearl of great price. (Matthew 13:46a)

Though he sought numerous pearls, he found one that surpassed any that he had found or would find. He realized that the pearl he found was unlike any other. He recognized its uniqueness, and its value. All else no longer mattered.

As Christians, we must remember

that we have the ONE PEARL that is more precious than anything else. Mary, the sister of Lazarus and Martha, understood this.

> *And she had a sister called Mary, which also sat at Jesus' feet, and heard his word. (Luke 10:39)*

When Jesus visited their home, she would stop all activities to sit at his feet. Does your relationship with God cause you to lay all activities down to pray and commune with Him?

Sold All and Bought

The merchant in this parable, like

the man in the first, sold all that he had and bought the pearl of great price. In this parable, the merchant's selling and buying clarifies how valuable the kingdom of heaven should be to us.

> *...went and sold all that he had and bought it. (Matthew 13: 46a)*

As a merchant, he lived by buying, trading, and selling goods. This man gave up his way of life in order to possess the pearl. Though the pearl was valuable, the parable gives no indication that he would sell it. Else, he would not have sold all that he had to get it.

The merchant man risked his livelihood for one pearl. In addition, he had to sell any other pearls and goods he possessed to buy it. We should be willing to risk and lose our lives for the kingdom of God. In doing so, we demonstrate its value.

I Will Open My Mouth in Parables

Notes:

I Will Open My Mouth in Parables

-Lesson 4-
The Value of the Kingdom of God

I Will Open My Mouth in Parables

From the parables of the hidden treasure and pearl, we discover the value of the kingdom of God. However, we have to address the question, "What makes the kingdom of God valuable? In order to appreciate its value, this has to be explored.

The kingdom of God comes with certain benefits. Each of them raises the value of the kingdom. Though there are numerous factors that contribute to the kingdom's value, we will explore seven.

Salvation

Entrance into the kingdom of God

brings men into salvation.

The greatest benefit of the kingdom is the salvation of the souls of men.

Jesus answered, Verily, verily, I say unto thee, Except a man be born of water and of the Spirit, he cannot enter into the kingdom of God. (John 3:5)

Salvation through Jesus brings us into the kingdom of God. Then, as partakers of the kingdom of God, we are saved from the judgment to come upon the face of the earth.

Eternal Life

The salvation offered in the kingdom leads to eternal salvation or eternal life. The kingdom is valuable because no price can be placed on eternal security.

And this is the promise that he hath promised us, even eternal life. (I John 2:25)

Salvation is only offered through Christ and His kingdom. Yet, if we receive Him, we will spend eternity in His presence.

Freedom from Sin

As members of the kingdom of God, we escape the kingdom of Satan.

Satan controls men through sin, which works death.

> *Forasmuch then as the children are partakers of flesh and blood, he also himself likewise took part of the same; that through death he might destroy him that had the power of death, that is, the devil. (Hebrews 2:14)*

However, when we enter into the kingdom of heaven, the power of sin is broken in our lives.

> *But God be thanked, that ye were the servants of sin, but ye have obeyed*

from the heart that form of doctrine which was delivered you. Being then made free from sin, ye became the servants of righteousness. (Romans 6:17-18)

We no longer have to be bound by ungodly habits, lusts, and desires. We have the power to deny the temptations of the flesh and the devil.

Righteousness

Through the kingdom of God, we become righteous. We inherit two forms of righteousness. The first is *positional* righteousness. Once we have believed on the Lord Jesus, we are righteous because of our faith.

> *For with the heart man believeth unto righteousness; and with the mouth confession is made unto salvation. (Romans 10:10)*

Our righteous standing before the Lord is secured. In addition to *positional* righteousness, we are able to develop *conditional* righteousness.

> *If ye know that he is righteous, ye know that every one that doeth righteousness is born of him. (I John 2:29)*

We are able to walk uprightly because we are the children of the kingdom of God. God considers us righteous and we will walk in righteousness.

Joy

Another product of the kingdom of God is joy. Joy comes from experiencing freedom from sin, guilt, condemnation, and shame.

There is therefore now no condemnation to them which are in Christ Jesus, who walk not after the flesh, but after the

Spirit. (Romans 8:1)

In addition, it grows as understanding of the reward of eternal life comes into focus. Moreover, it comes from the personal relationship with the Lord Jesus Christ.

Whom having not seen (that is, Jesus), ye love; in whom, though now ye see him not, yet believing, ye rejoice with joy unspeakable and full of glory. (I Peter 1:8 Parenthesis Mine)

We have joy knowing that He is our Helper. We can endure all things.

Peace

One of the greatest components of the kingdom of heaven is peace. Through the kingdom, we have peace with God.

Therefore being justified by faith, we have peace with God through our Lord Jesus Christ. (Romans 5:1)

We are no longer enemies, but friends. In addition to this, the kingdom brings peace in the midst of life's problems and tribulations. Finally, the kingdom gives us the ability to be at peace with others.

Power

The kingdom of God is not only experienced in word, but in power. God's power is available to us through the presence of the Holy Spirit.

Now the God of hope fill you with all joy and peace in believing, that ye may abound in hope, through the power of the Holy Ghost. (Romans 15:13)

For the kingdom of God is not in word, but in power. (I Corinthians 4:20)

He enables us to accomplish His will

through His power. The kingdom of God helps us to recognize His power and be channels of the same.

The above characteristics of the kingdom of God make it invaluable. Because of this, we can understand the responses of the men in the parables. If we keep these attributes of the kingdom in mind, they will help us to recognize and respond to its value.

I Will Open My Mouth in Parables

Notes:

I Will Open My Mouth in Parables

I Will Open My Mouth in Parables

-Study 2-
The Unmerciful Servant

(Lessons concerning Forgiveness)

I Will Open My Mouth in Parables

I Will Open My Mouth in Parables

-Lesson 1-
The Choice

Life is full of choices. Each day, we make hundreds of choices without second thought. Certain decisions are easy to make. Others prove to be difficult for a variety of reasons. As believers, we are consistently challenged to make sound, Christ-centered decisions in life.

The Obvious Choice

Among those decisions is the choice to forgive. Yes. Forgiveness is a choice. Regardless of the offence, Jesus commanded His followers to forgive. It may be difficult, but it can be done through Jesus Christ.

I can do all things through Christ which strengtheneth me. (Philippians 4:13)

Luke records some of Jesus' teachings on the issue of forgiveness in his gospel.

Take heed to yourselves: If thy brother trespass against thee, rebuke him; and if he repent, forgive him. And if he trespass against thee seven times in a day, and seven times in a day turn again to thee, saying, I repent; thou shalt forgive him. (Luke 17:3-4)

Jesus tells them to forgive the same person who offends seven times in a day. He was not promoting that after the seventh offense, forgiveness was to be withdrawn. His use of seven (being God's number of completion) expresses that however many times forgiveness is needed to bring peace between one and his brother, it should be offered.

In his gospel, Matthew gives a qualifying account of Jesus' teaching on forgiveness. It reveals the responsibility of the believer to forgive. After Jesus' transfiguration and their failure to deliver the demon-possessed boy, the disciples came to Jesus asking about who is the greatest in the kingdom of heaven.

In His response, Jesus brought up the issue of responding to a brother's offence (Matthew 18:15). Following the discourse, Peter asks a question,

> *Then came Peter to him, and said, Lord, how oft shall my brother sin against me, and I forgive him? Till seven times? (Matthew 18:21)*

Peter wanted to know if there was a limit to forgiveness. However, the Lord's response reveals the answer.

Jesus saith unto him, I say not unto thee, Until seven times: but, Until seventy times seven. (Matthew 18:22)

The Overwhelming Command

Jesus said that one was not only to forgive seven times, but seventy times seven. He is promoting unlimited forgiveness. To illustrate His statement about forgiveness, Jesus used the parable of the unmerciful servant.

Therefore is the kingdom of heaven likened unto a certain king, which would take account of his servants. And when he had begun to reckon, one was brought unto him, which owed him ten thousand talents. But forasmuch as he had not to pay, his lord commanded him to be sold, and his wife, and children and all that he had, and payment to be made. The servant therefore fell down, and worshipped him, saying, Lord, have patience with me, and I will pay thee all. Then the lord of that servant was moved with compassion, and loosed him, and forgave him the debt. But the same servant went out, and found one of his fellowservants, which owed him an hundred pence: and he laid hands on him, and took him by the throat, saying, Pay me that thou owest. And his fellowservant fell down at his feet, and besought him, saying, Have patience with me, and I will pay thee all. And he would not: but went and cast him into prison, till he should pay the debt. So when his fellowservants saw what was done, they were very sorry, and came and told unto their lord all that was done. Then his lord, after that he had called him, said unto him, O thou wicked servant, I forgave thee all that debt, because thou desiredst me: Shouldest not thou also have had compassion on thy fellowservant, even as I had pity on thee? And his lord was wroth, and delivered him to the tormentors, till he should pay all that was due unto him. So likewise shall my heavenly Father do also unto you, if ye from your hearts forgive not every one his brother their trespasses. (Matthew 18:23-35)

Jesus opens the parable by declaring this is what the kingdom of heaven is like. Whoever receives Jesus Christ becomes a member of the kingdom of heaven. He is under the rule and reign of God. Thus, this parable expresses how forgiveness is to be administered in the kingdom. As we consider this parable, we shall learn some invaluable lessons in forgiveness.

I Will Open My Mouth in Parables

Notes:

I Will Open My Mouth in Parables

-Lesson 2-
The Characters

I Will Open My Mouth in Parables

To begin our study, we want to identify the characters in this parable. Each is important to its understanding and application. Within this parable, the key figures are the *king*, the *servant*, the *fellowservant*, the other *fellowservants*, and the *tormentors*. These characters not only bring definition to Jesus' parable, but also to ourselves.

The King

Jesus opens the parable by mentioning a certain king. Who was this king? This is not important. However, Jesus' use of king is not arbitrary. He used the title of king to denote authority, power, rule, and judgment. Whatever qualities and abilities any given king possess were to be brought into mind throughout the rest of this parable.

> *Therefore is the kingdom of heaven likened unto a certain king, which would take account of his servants. (Matthew 18:23)*

The Application: The unnamed king in this parable is used to represent God, who is the Supreme Ruler. There are many names used to describe God, none of which defines the totality of His being.

Thus, the unnamed king is a reflection of the unsearchable God.

> *Hast thou not known? Hast thou not heard, that the everlasting God, the Lord, the Creator of the ends of the earth, fainteth not, neither is weary? There is no searching of his understanding. (Isaiah 40:28)*

The Servant

The next key figure in the parable is the servant. The text gives no precise indication of what the responsibilities of this servant were. However, if viewed in light of some other parables, it may be inferred that this servant's duties included some financial responsibilities. This may be the reason for the great debt that had accumulated.

> *And when he had begun to reckon, one was brought unto him, which owed him ten thousand talents. (Matthew 18:24)*

The Application: The servant in this parable represents the Christian. In this parable, his specific duties are not identified to communicate the universality of the central theme. This teaches that what happened to this servant can happen to any servant of God.

Then Peter opened his mouth, and said, Of a truth I perceive that God is no respecter of persons. (Acts 10:34)

Regardless of your status, office, church duties, and ministry, the message of the parable has to be received.

The Fellowservant

After being introduced to the servant, we are then informed of the debt of one of his fellowservants. The term fellowservant denotes that he and this person had essentially the same status before the king. He is also without any significant identification or role.

> *But the same servant went out and found one of his fellowservants. (Matthew 18:28a)*

The Application: The fellowservant represents any believer in the Body of Christ. It also denotes that before the king (meaning God) we are all the same.

> *I charge thee before God, and the Lord Jesus Christ, and the elect angels, that thou observe these things without preferring one before*

another, doing nothing by partiality. (I Timothy 5:21)

If one is a pastor and the other is an usher, the responsibilities of the kingdom apply to all. There is to be no hierarchy in terms of respect and demonstration of Christian conduct.

The Other Fellowservants

The other fellowservants, were concerned for the welfare of the fellowservant who was mistreated.

So, when his fellowservants saw what was done, they were very sorry. (Matthew 18:31a)

The Application: The other fellowservants, again, represent other Christians. They expressed love and concern for the wronged fellowservant. Believers have to be compassionate, willing to strive for justice and judgment among others in the Church.

> *By this shall all men know that ye are my disciples, if ye have love one to another. (John 13:35)*

They reflect the love and concern that believers should have for one another. This is how we demonstrate that we are Christ's disciples. We are not disciples by how we love the world through our good works. We verify our relationship with Christ through our love for others in the Body of Christ.

The Tormentors

The tormentors make their debut at the end of the parable. They were given authority to torture and to inflict pain upon the servant. They were able to do this until this servant somehow paid the debt that he owed the king.

And his lord was wroth, and delivered him to the tormentors. (Matthew 18:34a)

The Application: The tormentors in this parable represent guilt, shame, condemnation, and possibly eternal death. When a believer does not walk in obedience to the Lord, there may be consequences.

When Israel disobeyed God, their enemies triumphed over them. God delivers us from guilt, shame, and the like when we accept Jesus.

However, if we are not good servants, these may be allowed to have place in us. This is because the enemy gains access through sin.

Neither give place to the devil. (Ephesians 4:27)

Understanding the characters and how they are significant to Christians today, prepares us to comprehend Jesus' essential message.

I Will Open My Mouth in Parables

Notes:

I Will Open My Mouth in Parables

-Lesson 3-
The Circumstances

I Will Open My Mouth in Parables

The circumstances, which contributed to the central message of the parable, teach believers the importance of forgiveness in the kingdom of heaven. The circumstances in this parable involve the call, the cry, the compassion, the corruption, and the capture.

The Call

Jesus begins the parable with a certain king who decides to review the records of his servants.

> *Therefore is the kingdom of heaven likened unto a certain king, which would take account of his servants.*

And when he had begun to reckon, one was brought unto him, which owed him ten thousand talents. (Matthew 18:23-24)

After the records were checked, it was discovered that one of the servants owed ten thousand talents. For this time, this was an enormous amount of money. In response to this, the servant was brought before the king. It was time for him to pay his debt.

The Call Today. The servant came before the king to pay a debt. In the scriptures, our sins are referred to as debts in the

Lord's Prayer.

> *And forgive us our debts, as we forgive our debtors. (Matthew 6:12)*

When one sins, there is a breach in the relationship with God. Though Christ has made the atonement for sin, it still has to be confessed when committed. Thus, when we sin, we become indebted to God. When David committed his sins with Bathsheba, he stated that he sinned against God only.

> *Against thee, thee only, have I sinned, and done this evil in thy sight: that thou mightest be justified*

when thou speakest, and be clear when thou judgest. (Psalm 51:4)

The Christian repays his 'debt' through the confession of his sins. When this is done, he no longer is a candidate for the penalty of sin.

My little children, these things write I unto you, that ye sin not. And if any man sin, we have an advocate with the Father, Jesus Christ the righteous. (I John 2:1)

Some teach that once one is saved, he can live as he wants to. This is simply not true. A righteous life must accompany one's belief in Jesus. Thus, when one sins, confession and repentance is needed to continue in the righteousness that was received by faith. The king called for a repayment and God still calls believers to repentance.

The Cry

The servant did not have the money to repay the debt. The king commanded that he, his family, and his possessions be sold for repayment.

But forasmuch as he had not to pay, his lord commanded him to be sold, and his wife, and children, and all that he had, and payment to be made. (Matthew 18:25)

The man was taken into custody. He was to be put in debtor's prison. He and all that he had were to be sold for repayment. However, he cried out to the king for mercy.

The servant therefore fell down, and worshipped him, saying, Lord, have patience with me, and I will pay thee all. (Matthew 18:26)

The servant fell down before the king and made a heart-felt plea for patience. He expressed his intentions, if given more time, to repay the debt.

The Cry Today. Like this servant, the believer has to come to God in sincerity and truth. The servant cried out from his heart because of the debt.

> *And ye shall seek me, and find me, when ye shall search for me with all your heart. (Jeremiah 29: 13)*

When we sin, our confession cannot be with the lips only, but it has to be from the heart. This is the only way we can receive forgiveness.

The Compassion

After the servant's sincere cry, the

king responded. It is evident that the king perceived the sincerity and sorrow of the servant.

> *Then the lord of that servant was moved with compassion, and loosed him, and forgave him the debt. (Matthew 18:27)*

Seeing his display of emotion, the king was moved with compassion. He released the man from custody. In addition, he forgave him the debt. The king's compassion was so great that he gave the servant more than what he asked for.

The Compassion Today. The great compassion of the king reflects the compassion of God. During His earthly ministry, Jesus was moved by compassion frequently. The compassion of this king serves as a reminder of God's compassion for man.

> *Like as a father pitieth (has compassion on) his children, so the Lord pitieth them that fear him. For he knoweth our frame; he remembereth that we are dust. (Psalm 03:13-14 Parenthesis mine)*

He knows our frames. God knows

that man is vulnerable to sin. Because of this, He offers continual forgiveness even after one comes to Him through Jesus. He wants man to remain free from sin.

The Corruption

The servant was given more than time; his debt was erased. However, after such a display of emotion, the servant proved that he could be heartless. One of his fellowservants owed him some money.

The debt he owed the king would be tens of thousands by today's standard. Yet, his fellowservant owed him one hundred pence, which would only be between ten and twenty dollars by today's standards.

> *But the same servant went out, and found one of his fellowservants, which owed him an hundred pence: and he laid hands on him, and took him by the throat, saying, Pay me that thou owest. (Matthew 18:28)*

The servant, who had just received forgiveness for an enormous debt demonstrated cruelty to someone who was in the same situation as he was. The verse states that he found his fellowservant. This implies he searched for him with the intent to demand repayment.

The fellowservant could not pay him, at that time, and cried out to him for patience. Nevertheless, we see the forgetfulness and corruption of the main servant.

And his fellow servant fell down at his feet, and besought him, saying, Have patience with me, and I will pay thee all. And he would not: but went and cast him into prison, till he should pay the debt. (Matthew 18:29-30)

The fate that he had escaped, he inflicted upon someone who did not owe him much of anything. The money owed to him would not make a difference in his life or financial situation. However, he responded to his fellowservant as if he owed millions. This reveals his lack of love and compassion. In addition, it revealed his unappreciation for the favor that he had been shown.

The Corruption Today. The servant was unwilling to forgive his fellowservant. Though this situation is hypothetical, it reveals something important for believers.

The difference in the debts that were owed reflects our lifetime of sin before God as opposed to singular infractions from others.

Through Jesus, we are forgiven for a lifetime of sin and evil doings. If someone sins against us repeatedly, their sin against us will not measure up to our sins before God.

This fact should cause believers to be more forgiving of others. The way God forgave us is how we are to forgive others. This part of the parable should cause the Christian to examine himself.

Examine yourselves, whether ye be in the faith; prove your own selves. Know ye not your own selves, how that Jesus Christ is in you, except ye be reprobates? (2 Corinthians 13:5)

If it is extremely difficult for a Christian to forgive, there is corruption somewhere in them. Though offenses will come and some will be great, the Christian still has to be able to forgive. If Christ has forgiven us, we know what it feels like to be in debt and experience freedom. We should be willing to do the same for others.

The Capture

After these events, other fellowservants saw what was done and were grieved. They could not believe that the servant who had been relieved of great debt would mistreat his fellowservant.

So when his fellowservants saw what was done, they were very sorry, and came and told unto their lord all that was done. (Matthew 18:31)

The other fellowservants reported what was done. The servant had to go back before the king. The king was appalled by this servant's behavior.

> *Then his lord, after that he had called him, said unto him, O thou wicked servant, I forgave thee all that debt, because thou desiredst me: Shouldest not thou also have had compassion on thy fellowservant, even as I had pity on thee? And his lord was wroth, and delivered him to the tormentors, till he should pay all that was due unto him. (Matthew 18:32-34)*

He had been forgiven much, but he had not forgiven little. Thus, the king's original decree was revoked and the man was delivered to tormentors until he paid his debt.

The Capture Today. Believers have to remember the lifetime of sin from which they were freed. They have to be appreciative. If not, the freedom that God granted through Christ may be frustrated.

In this parable, the servant became a debtor again because of the wickedness of his heart. If a believer demonstrates this type of unforgiveness, he is walking in the way of sinners.

God is love. Those who have received Him, receive His capacity to love and forgive. Therefore, if a Christian cannot forgive, it points to a problem in their relationship with the Lord. If it is not resolved, the result may be a return to old ways and habits.

> *But now, after that ye have known God, or rather are known of God, how turn ye again to the weak and beggarly elements, whereunto ye desire again to be in bondage? (Galatians 4:9)*

If one cannot forgive, it is a problem

with the heart. It is in our hearts that we receive Christ. Christ and unforgiveness cannot dwell equally in one's heart. Eventually, one of the two will take the preeminence. Like the servant, one may be delivered over to the tormentors.

Notes:

I Will Open My Mouth in Parables

-Lesson 4-
The Conclusion

I Will Open My Mouth in Parables

To conclude the parable, Jesus makes a final statement that sums up the message of the story.

So likewise shall my heavenly Father do also unto you, if ye from your hearts forgive not everyone his brother their trespasses. (Matthew 18:35)

Jesus plainly stated that what happened to the servant would happen to those who did not forgive others.

God's Standard for Forgiveness

There is no room for any other interpretations. However, as with all things, God reserves the right to do what He wants. Some Christians do have a problem with forgiveness. Yet, if they are asking God for help in this matter, they will not suffer the fate of the servant.

The servant was judged fiercely because, in his heart, he was wicked. He did not see any problem with what he had done. This is not the same for believers who want to forgive, but struggle at times.

Man's Reasons for Unforgiveness

Jesus declared that forgiveness was the duty of the believer. Any believer who disregards this command stands in danger of God's judgment. This is not to scare believers, but give them a proper perspective on how to handle offenses.

Having established God's requirement, we do know that some struggle with forgiveness for various reasons. Here are three common reasons:

1. **They have been hurt repeatedly by the same person doing the same things.** In spite of this, Jesus stated that forgiveness was to be offered for repeat offenders.

2. **The pain inflicted was great.** Some have been abused (physically, sexually,

and emotionally). These types of wounds run deep. Yet, if one is willing to let it go, God will give strength so His command will not be violated because of the pain.

3. **Others feel that people do not deserve it.** God is the ONLY JUDGE. The Christian has to remember that no one deserved God's forgiveness, but He granted it.

As His disciples, we have to do the same. Regardless of the reason for struggling with unforgiveness, Jesus' warning supersedes a person's experiences.

The parable came to reinforce Jesus' command to forgive. In addition, it came to remind man of the unlimited forgiveness received from God after coming to Christ.

We have to make sure we do not be as the servant in this parable but reflect the compassion of God to others. This is to be done even in times of great affliction and offense.

To conclude our examination of forgiveness, we have listed scriptures exhorting Christians to forgive. If you are having difficulty, apply the following scriptures with prayer and humility for victory over offenses and unforgiveness.

And be ye kind one to another, tenderhearted, forgiving one another, even as God for Christ's sake hath forgiven you. (Ephesians 4:32)

For if ye forgive men their trespasses, your heavenly Father will also forgive you: But if ye forgive not men their trespasses, neither will your Father forgive your trespasses. (Matthew 6:14-15)

And when ye stand praying, forgive, if ye have ought against any: that your Father also which is in heaven may forgive you your trespasses. But if ye do not forgive, neither will your Father which is in heaven forgive your trespasses. (Mark 11:25-26)

Judge not, and ye shall not be judged: condemn not, and ye shall not be condemned: forgive, and ye shall be forgiven. (Luke 6:37)

Blessed are the merciful: for they shall obtain mercy. (Matthew 5:7)

Put on therefore, as the elect of God, holy and beloved, bowels of mercies, kindness, humbleness of mind, meekness, longsuffering; Forbearing one another, and forgiving one another, if any man have a quarrel against any: even as Christ forgave you, so also do ye. (Colossians 3:12-13)

Remember, all things are possible to them that believe. Jesus taught forgiveness. But we have to be willing to forgive. This is achieved by remembering the forgiveness that we have received.

Again, Jesus' parable came as an exhortation and warning to those who followed Him.

Notes

I Will Open My Mouth in Parables

Bibliography

Merriam-Webster Online Dictionary. Copyright © 2005 by Merriam-Webster, Incorporated. All rights reserved.

The Bible Library. Copyright 1988 – 2000. Ellis Enterprises Incorporated, 4205 McAuley Blvd., Suite 385, Oklahoma City, OK 73120, (405) 749-0273. All Rights Reserved.

Lockman Foundation. *Comparative Study Bible.* Zondervan Publishing House. Grand Rapids, MI, c1984

Smith, William. *Smith's Bible Dictionary.* Holman Bible Publishers. Nashville, TN. c1994

I Will Open My Mouth in Parables

Notes

I Will Open My Mouth in Parables